DISCOVER 🐾 DOGS WITH
THE AMERICAN CANINE ASSOCIATION

ICA

INTERNATIONAL CANINE ASSOCIATION, INC.

"Tracking your pets around the world"

★ OFFICIAL SEAL ★ ®

ICA, a subdivision of ACA

I LIKE
LABRADOODLES!

Linda Bozzo

ICA, a subdivision of ACA

It is the Mission of the American Canine Association (ACA) to provide registered dog owners with the educational support needed for raising, training, showing, and breeding the healthiest pets expected by responsible pet owners throughout the world. Through our activities and services, we encourage and support the dog world in order to promote best-known husbandry standards as well as to ensure that the voice and needs of our customers are quickly and properly addressed.

Our continued support, commitment, and direction are guided by our customers, including veterinary, legal, and legislative advisors. ACA aims to provide the most efficient, cooperative, and courteous service to our customers and strives to set the standard for education and problem solving for all who depend on our services.

For more information, please visit www.acacanines.com, e-mail customerservice@acadogs.com, phone 1-800-651-8332, or write to the American Canine Association at PO Box 121107, Clermont, FL 34712.

Published in 2017 by Enslow Publishing, LLC.
101 W. 23rd Street, Suite 240, New York, NY 10011

Library of Congress Cataloging-in-Publication Data
Names: Bozzo, Linda.
Title: I like Labradoodles! / Linda Bozzo.
Description: New York, NY : Enslow Publishing, 2017. | Series: Discover dogs with the american canine association | Includes bibliographical references and index. | Audience: Ages 5 and up. | Audience: Grades K to 3.
Identifiers: LCCN 2016020286 | ISBN 9780766081710 (library bound) | ISBN 9780766081697 (pbk.) | ISBN 9780766081703 (6-pack)
Subjects: LCSH: Labradoodle--Juvenile literature.
Classification: LCC SF429.L29 B69 2017 | DDC 636.72/8--dc23
LC record available at https://lccn.loc.gov/2016020286

Printed in China

To Our Readers: We have done our best to make sure all websites in this book were active and appropriate when we went to press. However, the author and the publisher have no control over and assume no liability for the material available on those websites or on any websites they may link to. Any comments or suggestions can be sent by e-mail to customerservice@enslow.com.

Photo Credits: Cover, p. 1 KariDesign/Shutterstock.com; p. 3 (left) Picture-Pets/Shutterstock.com; p. 3 (right) Peter Louwers/Shutterstock.com; p. 5 © iStockphoto.com/s-eyerkaufer; p. 6 © ZUMA Press Inc/Alamy Stock Photo; p. 9 Hero Images/Getty Images; p. 10 Natasha Sioss/Moment Open/Getty Images; p. 13 (left) Don Mason/Corbis/Getty Images; p 13 (right) © iStockphoto.com/jclegg (collar), Luisa Leal Photography/Shutterstock.com (bed), gvictoria/Shutterstock.com (brush), In-Finity/Shutterstock.com (dishes), © iStockphoto.com/Lisa Thornberg (leash, toys); p. 14 David Joel/Photographer's Choice RF/Getty Images; p. 15 Tannis Toohey/Toronto Star/Getty Images; p. 17 LWA/Photographer's Choice/Getty Images; p. 18 LWA/Taxi/Getty Images; p. 21© Paul Brown/Alamy Stock Photo; p. 22 The Dog Photographer/Shutterstock.com.

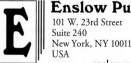

Enslow Publishing
101 W. 23rd Street
Suite 240
New York, NY 10011
USA
enslow.com

CONTENTS

IS A LABRADOODLE RIGHT FOR YOU?

Labradoodles make great family dogs. They are good with other dogs and pets.

Labradoodles are a designer breed. They are part Labrador retriever and part poodle.

A DOG OR A PUPPY?

Labradoodles are very smart. This makes them easy to train. If you do not have time to train a puppy, an older Labradoodle may be better for your family.

Depending on their mix, Labradoodles can grow to be medium to large in size.

These gentle dogs are often used as guide, assistance, and therapy dogs.

LOVING YOUR LABRADOODLE

It is easy to love a Labradoodle. They are friendly and playful. You can love your Labradoodle by cuddling and playing with him.

EXERCISE

Labradoodles need lots of playtime and long walks on a **leash**. They are always ready to play games, like **fetch**.

FEEDING YOUR LABRADOODLE

Labradoodles can be fed wet or dry dog food. Ask a **veterinarian (vet)**, a doctor for animals, which food is best for your dog and how much to feed her.

Give your Labradoodle fresh, clean water every day.

Remember to keep your dog's food and water dishes clean. Dirty dishes can make a dog sick.

Do not feed your dog people food. It can make her sick.

Your new dog will need:

a collar with a tag

a bed

a brush

food and water dishes

a leash

toys

Labradoodles can have different kinds of coats, from straight to curly.

GROOMING

Some Labradoodles are like Labrador retrievers and **shed**. This means their hair fails out. Others are like poodles and shed little to none. All Labradoodles need to be brushed to keep them clean and looking their best.

Use a gentle soap made just for dogs.

Your dog will need a bath every so often. A Labradoodle's nails need to be clipped. A vet or **groomer** can show you how. Your dog's ears should be cleaned and his teeth should be brushed by an adult.

WHAT YOU SHOULD KNOW ABOUT LABRADOODLES

Labradoodles do best with a fenced-in yard to play in.

Because Labradoodles are a designer breed, each dog may be different.

Labradoodles are great for first-time pet owners.

You will need to take your new dog to the vet for a checkup. He will need shots, called vaccinations, and yearly checkups to keep him healthy. If you think your dog may be sick or hurt, call your vet.

A GOOD FRIEND

Labradoodles can be quiet yet playful friends to everyone they meet. They can live to up to fifteen years.

Labradoodles don't make good watchdogs because they are so friendly.

NOTE TO PARENTS

It is important to consider having your dog spayed or neutered when the dog is young. Spaying and neutering are operations that prevent unwanted puppies and can help improve the overall health of your dog.

It is also a good idea to microchip your dog, in case he or she gets lost. A vet will implant a microchip under the skin containing an identification number that can be scanned at a vet's office or animal shelter. The microchip registry is contacted and the company uses the ID number to look up your information from a database.

Some towns require licenses for dogs, so be sure to check with your town clerk.

For more information, speak with a vet.

There are many dogs, young and old, waiting to be adopted from animal shelters and rescue groups.

fetch To go after a toy and bring it back.

groomer A person who bathes and brushes dogs.

leash A chain or strap that attaches to a dog's collar.

shed When dog hair falls out so new hair can grow.

vaccinations Shots that dogs need to stay healthy.

veterinarian (vet) A doctor for animals.

Read About Dogs

Books

Edison, Emily. *You'll Love Labradoodles*. Mankato, MN.: Capstone Press, 2014.

Owen, Ruth. *Labradoodles*. New York, NY.: Power Kids Press, 2013.

Websites

American Canine Association Inc., Kids Corner
acakids.com
Visit the official website of the American Canine Association.

National Geographic for Kids, Pet Central
kids.nationalgeographic.com/explore/pet-central/
Learn more about dogs and other pets at the official site of the National Geographic Society for Kids.

INDEX